Dear mom,
This is a fun book
to read every day as you
start out. The reflections
are simple yet profound
enjoy love
Annette

To my husband

Grains
of Wheat

by Kelly B. Kelly

*Illustrations by
Jacqueline Seitz*

LIVING FLAME PRESS
LOCUST VALLEY, N.Y. 11560

Third printing 1983

Cover: Robert Manning

ISBN: 0-914544-32-2

Published by: Living Flame Press, Box 74, Locust Valley, N.Y. 11560

Printed in the United States of America

GRAINS OF WHEAT

Unless a wheat grain falls on the ground
and dies
it remains only a single grain;
but if it dies,
it yields a rich harvest.

John 12:24

PREFACE

I am not the spiritual type. Never have been.
Church-goer, yes — from twenty on, but not
much at praying or reading the Bible or taking
time to be alone with the Lord. No need to. I
could handle it all by myself. I thought. My action
shaped my life. I thought. The successes of my
life were my doing. I thought.

Then one day in May six years ago, I looked in
the mirror and did not like what I saw. How could
I, who could handle everything just fine and
whose life was full of good things, have a face so
tense, anxious, and full of despair? Why did I
never experience deep joy, serenity, peace? Why
was the solution I sought always ahead of me
some place and never in my grasp? In spite of all
the years of straining to do right, to be right?

In my heart of hearts I seemed to know that
the answer to my questions lay in God. I had
thought I had Him but I must have misplaced Him
somehow. Then I began to shift direction by
consciously and humbly seeking the Lord.
Realizing I couldn't handle my life. Admitting I
needed the Lord. I prayed more, read more,
talked to a spiritual friend. By the following
winter I was keeping a spiritual journal and in the
spring I joined a group for prayer. Then I began to
change slowly in my heart and the following fall I
turned my life over to Jesus.

That is how my journey with Jesus into the
inner kingdom began. That kingdom is God's and I

found that once I began that journey toward Him, anything could happen. My life has been full of surprises. God may not have given me what I wanted or what I felt I needed, but He has never bored me! And He has given me some spiritual experiences that I never would have believed could happen to a practical, factual, organized and secular person like myself.

So in the spring of 1977 I began to write down what I felt the Father was telling me in prayer. These were teachings to lead, correct, inspire, and encourage me in my often faltering walk with Jesus. Many times I needed the same simple lesson over and over. Often I did not understand why I wrote what I did or what it meant. Usually I understood it later when circumstances drove it through my thick head. Frequently I completely failed to follow His guidance and in sorrow had to begin all over again.

After a year or so, and if the occasion seemed appropriate, I began to read a few of these teachings to others. Their response was encouraging. And when I was led to Ecclesiasticus 41:14 in prayer:

"Wisdom hidden away and treasure undisplayed, what use are either of these?"

it seemed the Lord wanted me to share them with others. From then on, the matter seemed to be taken out of my hands and now I want only to remain out of sight and let the Lord do His work unimpeded.

The first encouraging response that He would do just that in others was the reaction of the secretary who typed them for the publisher. She worked at night, after her regular job, and reported that inevitably what she typed at night seemed to answer a particular situation she had encountered that day. More than once, when my awful handwriting was unreadable and she had to give up for the night, the teaching she had found impossible to read would seem perfectly legible the next night. Furthermore it would answer a problem she had encountered that day and not the day before.

I pray then that the Lord will use these insights in your life too. You are different from me and I am sure He will use them differently in your life. The beauty of the Lord's work is that the same gift from Him can be used in so many different ways for so many different people. And with delight in that fact, I pray,

"May He bless you to the limit that your heart can hold — and then increase your heart to hold more blessings than you ever dreamed of!"

K.B. Kelly, October 1980

CONTENTS

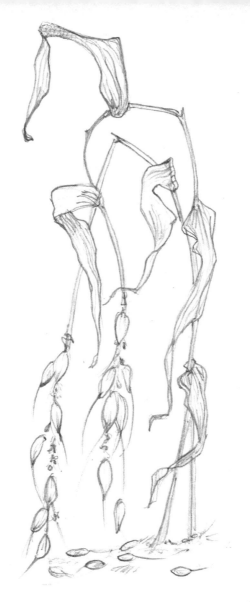

THE FALLEN GRAIN

Very powerful —

O GLORIOUS APOSTLE, St. Jude Thaddeus, true relative of Jesus and Mary, I salute you through the Most Sacred Heart of Jesus! Through this Heart I praise and thank God for the graces He has bestowed upon you. Humbly prostrate before you, I implore you through this Heart to look down upon me with compassion. Oh, despise not my poor prayers; let not my trust be confounded! To you God has granted the privilege of aiding mankind in the most desperate cases. Oh, come to my aid, that I may praise the mercies of God! All my life I will be grateful to you and will be your faithful client until I can thank you in Heaven. Amen.

Blessed Apostle with confidence we invoke you! *(Three Times)*

St. Jude, Help of the Hopeless, aid me in my distress! *(Three Times)*

Shrine of Saint Jude

Dominican Fathers

183 Bayview Avenue
Jersey City, N.J. 07305

PRAYER

O Almighty Father,

You have touched my heart so often with what you have taught me in prayer. You have calmed my confusion, given direction to my wanderings, and steadied me when I felt panicky. You have patiently taught me the lesson again and again when I failed to follow. You have put up with me when I was only lukewarm and waited till I was ready to listen before giving me the word I needed. You did not condemn me when I turned my back on you but with tact and kindness put me back on the track. You even taught me to laugh at myself!

You have calmed me, strengthened me, encouraged me, and lifted me into the wind and the sunlight. You have filled me and given me peace.

Dear Father, when you led me to the scripture that said: Wisdom hidden away and treasure undisplayed, what use are either of these? (Ecclesiasticus 41:14)

I understood it to mean that you would have me share with others the words you have given me in prayer. They are my treasure and with a thankful heart I ask you to bless them so that, like the transformation of the seed in the ground and the silent passage of roots, they may propagate your truth and manifest your life wherever they are planted.

Thank you, Father, for your love. Amen.

PRAYER

Father in heaven —

I'm so sick of listening to my own voice. Enter into me and cast out superfluous clutter, the spiritual chaos. Knock down my walls. Reach for my rigid heart, surrounded with defenses of self-righteousness and invulnerability and break into it. Turn the hardness of my heart into warmth and softness, beating in harmony with your rhythm. Deliver me from pretentiousness, from aloofness, from coldness and from fear. Let me dare to be vulnerable — naked in your light. I am a fool to pretend that I've got my act together. Your Son sees right through people like me.

Let His eyes pierce me now. I will not be afraid of His scrutiny because I know that behind it is love. Let me be touched deeply by His love today — open and vulnerable. Oh Father, I throw myself on the fire of His love. I trust Him to purify and rebuild me.

Oh help me, Father, I need renewal!

MY LOVING HEART

My child:

When you trust me with all your heart, you will learn of my wonders. I will teach you what was hidden to you before. Do not wonder at what I tell you. Just place your heart in mine, in trust, and I will place in your mind what you need to know.

There is so much I want to tell you. Keep trying to have a pure heart so that I can share my wonders with you. A pure heart is receptive to my teaching. Reject any dross as soon as it accumulates and you will be free to learn from me. Be open as a flower is to the sun and I will pour the rays of caring concern and wisdom on you. Know that I want to do this because of my great love for you.

My love for the souls I have created is so great, you cannot comprehend it. I want to share my gifts with all people who will accept them. My greatest joy would be to send a constant flow of wisdom and knowledge and love into every heart on earth. Many hearts are closed to me.

Give me joy by opening your heart to me and inspiring many other hearts to open to me, too. Then, trust me to do my great work in you and in other souls. My passion for souls knows no bounds. You will be pierced by my limitless love. Do not be afraid. Trust my loving heart.

YOU ARE STARDUST

My child:

Draw near in the stillness of the night. In the silence of the stars, you will learn of my love for you. In the emptiness of space, you will discover my love. You are suspended in the enormity of my creation. You are as small as stardust, yet precious as a whole constellation in my eyes. You are loved with the same love that created galaxies. You, tiny child, are most precious of all that I have created. You are part of me — you are a part of my love — you are indivisible from me — you live in me — you are coming back to me. You are a mote, a flower; you are clay, a bird, an isopod in the sea. You are creation. You are beloved. You are mine. Open yourself to this knowledge. Do not be afraid to be loved. Open yourself to my love, in trust. The one who formed you wants only to complete you. Oh my child, live every moment in the awareness of my love for you.

RELEASE THE CLUTTER

My child:

Clear out the clutter of your heart. Empty yourself of non-essentials. Purify your thoughts and simplify your actions so that you can be a channel of my grace. Eat less, drink less, strive less. Pray more, read more, be still more.

Receiving my loving power is not complicated — it is instigated by emptying yourself of all that stands in the way — then you will feel the flow of my grace.

A child puts no restraints on its parents' love but accepts that love fully. This is how I would have you be — willing to set aside the world and accept my tremendous love for you.

I know all the complications of your life — every one. Sin and circumstance have placed many stumbling blocks in your way. Believe that these can be set aside by your diligence. The rewards are greater than you can imagine.

Release the clutter and be filled. I want to fill your life to the fullest. I long to hold you close, fill you with the experience and the joy of my love.

ACCEPTANCE OF MY WAY

My child:

My ways are not your ways. My action moves upon the earth sometimes in totally unrecognized ways. If you puzzle or worry or rebel against happenings, you will waste your commitment to me. Everything, good or bad, that befalls you has a place in my plan. You cannot know how or why. Your acceptance of my plan is an exercise in complete trust. When you turn to me in childlike trust, you free yourself to receive my power and my peace.

The way to my Kingdom is simple. Shake off the worldliness that becomes attached to you as a lamb shakes snow from its coat. Shake the snow aside and come to me in stillness every day, and indeed whenever more snow accumulates. In stillness with me, in absolute surrender to my will, you will find peace and strength and all the gifts of my spirit that you will need in your life. I am your Father, your Abba, and I love to pour my blessing on you.

YOU ARE DOUGH

My child:

You are dough and of you I will make my bread. With my hands I will knead you, pummel you and blend you. I will let you rise, then work you anew, whereupon you will rise once more, only to be worked down again. Finally, I will bake you, and in the furnace of my love you will be transformed. You will emanate a fragrance and your texture will no longer be heavy but light and airy. Then you will give nourishment to others. The raw ingredients of flour and eggs and water and yeast will be transformed into vital food which will sustain life. Do not cling to your old self. Let go the ingredients of your personality and I will make a new creation of you. A baker handles his ingredients with loving care so that his bread will not be heavy or bruised. How much more lovingly will I deal with you! Trust my caring hands. I will keep you from all harm. You are mine and precious to me beyond your imagining.

THE SHINING WEB

My child:

I want to draw you closer to me. I want you to be touched in every facet of your life by the filaments of my love. I am light. I am air. I am a spun web of love sparkling with brightness. I am touchable. I am untouchable. I am nebulous. I am the sureness of your existence. I am within you. I transcend your being.

I want to permeate every fiber of your body, every cranny of your mind. I want to sustain and uplift you, to comfort and encourage you. I want to give you sureness of direction, protection against pitfalls. I want to glorify your vision. I want to give you a taste of eternal joy, a glimpse of eternal vistas, the root of eternal peace.

Open your heart to me. Hold out your open hands and I will fill them with my love. Oh, my child, rest in my shining web of love. You will never know such love as mine.

LOSING THE WAY

My child:

You lost your way. Your way is my way and you will never lose it by following me. To lose the way means that you cannot see the path to follow me and have no idea which way to go. How can you find your way? You must resort to prayer and surrender to me. Then, I will open your eyes and gently bring you back to the path. You will see that it was there all along and quite close to you although you faltered and could not find it.

I do not want you to falter. I give you the path and my word is the light to guide you on it. Pray, surrender, and read my word and you will not lose the path. Pray without ceasing, surrender your moments, read scripture often. Then you will have eyes to see the way always.

In love, I give you the way. In love, I guide you on it. In love, I will lead you to the end.

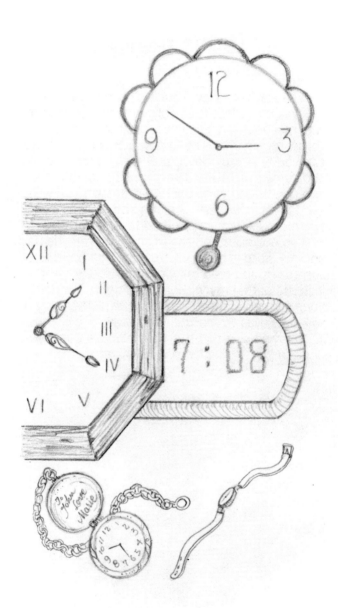

THE TICKING OF THE CLOCK

My child:

Free yourself from the inexorable ticking of the clock. I do not want you to cut and measure your day into small boxes of time. Nothing in my creation is so regimented. Even the sweep of day into night changes with the seasons and man cannot measure a year into small boxes. Nor can he time the motion of the tides to perfection.

Take a lesson from creation and allow me to move in harmony within your being, unhampered by the constriction of time. Do not be enslaved by minutes — time is mine, not yours. Be aware that when I enter into your life by your invitation, I must not be restricted by a schedule. Give me the freedom to work when and where I will. Give yourself the freedom to receive my grace. My love for you is timeless, my child. Absolutely infinite.

TURN THE STUBBLE UNDER

My child:

Beware that your spiritual life has seasons of growth and rest as does the earth.

Bring in the sheaves before it rains. Do not let the harvest spoil. Distribute fruit among the needy. Do not store it in barns. Give all away. I will take care of your future needs.

Let the rains soak into the stubble soil. Let my living water refresh and revitalize the earth during its rest. Let the snow fall, the cold freeze, the sun bake. Let the stubble disintegrate in the weather until you can plow it under. Then, it will enrich and fertilize the soil for future crops. Be patient and do not rush this process. Many changes go on in the earth and they cannot be rushed.

Rest like the earth, for a time, my child. Let my living waters soak into you. Let the stubble rot, let the weeds and leaves break down. Spread the fertilizer of your effort to reach me on the surface of the ground. You will know when the earth is soft enough to be turned over for a new seeding. Then, it will bring forth abundant fruit and you will rejoice.

Then, there will be singing and dancing in the land and no one near you will go hungry. Then, you will experience the abundance of my love. And there will be enough for all — a bountiful harvest of virtue. Rejoice and give thanks.

SURRENDER THE TROOPS

My child:

I want to be the captain of your soul.

I want to do a work in you. But I am a jealous captain. I demand surrender of all your troops — all your soldiers of pride, resentment, coldness, discouragement, spiritual envy, self-righteousness, criticism, indifference. I ask you not to hold one back but to make me a gift of all of them. If one reappears in your rank, I ask you to surrender it again to me — and again, and again, and again. These soldiers will support you no more. Place no reliance on them.

I wish to be the captain of your soul, and when I am, I will lead you from victory to victory. Dare to trust me. Your rewards will be great. I shower riches on those whom I command. Come, stand before me and receive your blessing.

THE GOD OF SURPRISES

My child:

Out of indistinct clouds, I can form something solid and beautiful. I can dissolve that which exists so that it is no more. I can turn bad into good, tragedy into triumph, something hopeless into something so filled with promise that you wonder why you never saw it before.

Do not limit me in your thinking, my child. I am the God of surprises, turnabouts and miracles. I am the God of that which is unbelievable and unexplainable. All that is required is unlimited trust in me — trust in patience, trust in trial, trust filling your whole heart and mind.

If you cannot trust completely, be willing to ask for my help. Don't be afraid to call out, "Help thou my unbelief." I am your compassionate father and long to aid you. I need only your willing heart. Like a mother hen, I gather my children with willing hearts into my feathers each night. I restore and warm and encourage them. I give them rest from their fatigue, strength for their growth, heat when they grow cold.

Come into my feathers, little chick. You cannot fly yet. I will harbor and succor you every moment of your day. I provide for you, watch over you, and envelop you in my love. I cover you with sheltering wings.

SATURATE YOURSELF IN MY LOVE

My child:

I love you in every dust mote in a sunbeam. I love you in deep shade. I love you in every flower and blade of grass, in every hawk and feeble moth. I love you in sweat and strain and in silent moonlight. I love you in wind, I love you in cold, I love you in firelight and hidden places. I love you in the very air you breathe, every sight you see, every sound you hear. I surround your senses with the very fabric of love. I permeate your being and the world around you.

Saturate yourself in the evidence of my love for you. It is your heritage as my heir. You are my child and all that I have is yours. It is my joy to pour it upon you.

A parent knows this joy in a limited way. Imagine how much I, as your creator, am filled with the delight of pouring out my creative love on you. Be open to my flood of love. Bring others who thirst, to drink of the flood. My abundance extends to all. Drink deep of this nourishment, my child, and fill your life with my love.

DO NOT GO RUSHING BY

My child:

When you are hurt and wounded, when you are threatened by what you dislike, when you make no headway in your mastery of self, when your weakness engulfs you — then, my child, come softly into my waiting arms. In gentleness, I hold them wide. Too often, you go rushing by and fail to notice me. Things that hurt you or slow your progress force you to stop rushing and to see me, patiently waiting beside the way to comfort and sustain you.

Oh my child, I long to enfold you always. It grieves me that so often you are stiff and in constant motion when all is well.

Do not wait until disaster strikes before seeking me. Come and be company with me. Walk quietly with me. Sit in silence beside me. Let go a little precious time. Let it go completely and relax in my presence. Your time will not be lost — I will reward you. Joys you cannot imagine will be given to you in return for time ungrudgingly given to me.

Men cannot guess what benefits I have ready for those who seek my presence. If you passed a shop full of wonderous gifts that were yours just for spending a little time talking to the shopkeeper, would you go rushing by?

Surrender your time and your will. My love will reward you.

BE QUIET WITH ME

My child:

I love you. I love you with an immeasurable love. I hold you with tenuous threads. You are suspended in my care. Even in illness, tiredness, distress, you are in the gentle web of my custody. When you do not sense this, when you feel abandoned, fruitless, unable to function as a vessel of my love, take time to rest. Be quiet with me until you know my presence again.

Do not be anxious to do all the time. You will only wear yourself out. Just be — be in my presence, be in my light, be suspended in my care. Be wholly mine and what you do will take care of itself.

My saints never set out to conquer the world. They sought me first, each in his own way. They immersed themselves in my presence. Then, when they went out, they could not help but conquer the world, though it was an incidental by-product of their love for me.

You cannot know when what you do or say will be effective. You can only open yourself to me continually and I, working through you, will make your life effective. Your primary act of doing and being, your primary task, is to seek me.

He who seeks will find. Your act of knocking will open the door. I love you, my child, and invite you to be with me every day, all day long. After quiet communion with me you will feel my presence. Then how I will restore and refresh you and pour my love into you! Then you will truly be a vessel of my love!

LOVE IS THE UNDERGIRDING

My child:

Love is the central thread running through the fabric, holding it all together. Love is the foundation of the building, poured before construction was ever begun. Love is the deep soil in which the tree grows. Love is the undergirding of all my creation. Unseen, unrecognized, it is at the core of every creature's being, of the very earth itself. My creation would not exist without love. My creation is love itself.

Since I create you in love, can you then live and move and have your being without love? Since I give my very self to live and die for you, can you turn your back on love? Life without love is hell itself. It is life without me. I want you to live in love — to build on love — to be immersed in love — to contemplate my love for you so that the thought of love is ever present in your mind.

Do not be concerned about the unlovely characteristics you find in yourself. Fasten your attention on my love and as you grow in depth toward it, those characteristics will fade and diminish. Be resolute in turning away from the world and toward me — daily, hourly, moment by moment. My love is all you will ever need. I would enfold you in my heart. Come in, my child and grow in my love.

WALK IN THE SHADE

My child:

I love you so much. Be open to my love. Be pliant to my will. I know you have trouble running aground and that your will is strong. Do not worry. I have the means to overcome all problems. Trust me completely.

You are a child playing in a pathless field, picking flowers. Come out of the field. Take my hand and walk with me on a woodland path. Give me your flowers and delight in this new road. Though you will miss the sun, there is much loveliness where you are going. Flowers in the woodlands, though never as abundant as in a field, are more beautiful, more graceful, and more rare. Come, find the forest flowers with me. Hold my hand and you will never be afraid.

My love surrounds you like a cloud, a protective mist. Let it seep into every fiber of your being. Love, love, eternal love. Love never changing, never ending. Love in a million facets, love hidden, love blazing, love discovering, love with might, love in a breath of air. Delight in my love for you. Come, walk in the shade with me.

SIMPLIFY YOUR HEART

Dear child:

I want you to simplify your heart. I want you to take small steps. I want you to do only one thing at a time. I want you to be as single-hearted as a child.

Reduce your days to moments — small bunches of time. Approach each piece of time in wonder and trust. Consecrate it to me wholeheartedly and then, open the package to see what is contained within it. Then, go on to the next.

Pray one prayer at a time. Do an act of love for one person at a time. Talk to one person and give that person your whole attention and love. Face one problem at a time. Consider it deeply. Give it to me in prayer. Do what you decide, then leave it in my hands. Do not pick it up again.

There is a time for grieving, a time for rest, a time for laughing, a time for tears, a time for work, a time for travel, a time for action — but not all at once!

Be childlike in your approach. Trust me like a child. Love everyone you meet like a child. Shake off discouragement like a child. Put your hand in mine and walk joyfully with me, little one. You need do no more.

Be my simple, open-hearted trusting child. Don't be afraid. I am always with you.

COMFORTING LOVE

My child:

I place my arm around you and you feel my strength and warmth and are encouraged. I want you to do likewise to others.

Comfort my people! You know how often you need comfort. When you look at others, know that they are also in need of comforting love. Look for this need especially when someone is being harsh or overbearing to you. Follow my Son's example in seeing beyond people's faults into their hearts. Do not abandon them.

O my child, what a hunger there is in your life for the divine! You came from me and will come back to me. You need me all your life long. You need me when brashness covers your fear, when authoritativeness covers your insecurity, when crossness covers your fatigue, when the mask you wear covers the weakness within. These are all marks of your humanness.

To grow in me, to grow like the model I have sent you, you need to admit your humanity and ask for divine help. Do not let your pride stand in the way of a life of growth and glory.

Come to me, come to me my child! My arms are open wide to welcome you. I will hold you and hug you and never cast you away. My love will fill your every need. Humanity knows no love like mine. My love will fill your every need. Humanity knows no love like mine. My love will comfort you and take care of you forever. Come, claim my love, my little child.

DO NOT FIGHT THE THICKET

My child:

You are the epitome of a tired child. Your body aches, you feel weak and unable to begin another day. Things just seem too difficult to cope with. You have tried and failed. You are in a thicket too dense to see out of, confused, lonely, worn out.

You are not alone, little one. Do not fight the thicket. Call aloud for Jesus and He will come to you, right where you are. Turn your face toward Him. Thank Him and praise Him. Forget all else but that. Place your hand in His; feel His arm around your shoulder, and before you know it, you will approach the clearing, with little effort.

Do not strain to disentangle yourself. You will be scratched and bruised and exhausted in the process. Mine is an easier way through which you will emerge calm and refreshed.

Rejoice that my easier way is yours, that the struggle is not as great as you make it. Be willing to receive this blessing, little one, born of my love for you.

THE MIST AND THE MYSTERY

My child:

Though the way is misty and the sun is obscured, do not hesitate to take my hand and plunge ahead. Mystery demands courage and courage is the outward evidence of trust in me. Nothing can befall you which can harm or destroy you, if you rely on me. Fear of the unknown, of the mist and mystery, will knot your stomach and twist your thinking if you do not remember to focus on me. Turn your eyes to me and take my hand in trust every minute of your day.

When things are easy for you, practice the constant linking of your heart to mine, moment by moment, so that when hardship strikes, or hurt or pain or the unusual crisis, it will be ingrained in you to look at me first, before my plan or action is known in your mind. Then you will be safe.

My love for you is your safeguard in all things. Nothing can happen to you where my love will not shield you! Remain in my love and my presence, dear child, where you are safe at all times.

THE PEACEFUL HEART

My child:

A peaceful heart is the product of right living. You cannot cling to a thing that is wrong in your life and expect to have peace in your heart. Many desire the peace that surpasses understanding but cannot achieve it because they harbor something that is not in my will for them and cannot let it go.

To be honest enough to face everything in your life, even those things which aren't quite clean and pure, is the first step. To completely surrender those shady items to me in order to live in my will is the second step. It will follow that the great treasure of inner peace — peace which can never be shaken, taken from you or lost — will be my gift to you.

Peace is not plenty, not joy, not a loving emotion. It is not strength in crisis, nor certainty in thought and action. It is not freedom from doubt and despair. It is not a contemplative spirit or an abundance of charisma or supernatural wisdom. My gift of peace undergirds all these, shines at the core of your living, moving and being and provides the solid foundation of unity with me upon which you build all that you think and do and feel, every way in which you act and react. If you do not have peace in your heart, you cannot draw close to me. If you have my peace, an endless spiritual journey toward me opens before you. Peace be to you. My peace be with you. Not as the world gives do I give it to you. Come to me and I will give you my peace.

THE ROCK,
THE ANCHOR, THE REFUGE

My child:

I am the steadiness you seek. I am the rock, the anchor, the refuge. I am the Lord of order and peace. To be with me is to banish turmoil, anxiety, and confusion.

I stretch my arms out to the battered and storm-weary, to the exhausted, the stumbling, the anxious, and the lost. There is no other safe haven but within my arms. There is no lasting peace but within me. There is no security, no order, no love that endures but mine.

Step out of your disorder, confusion, anxiety, and spend some time with me. I want your time without constraint, so that I may truly speak to your heart. Do not look over your shoulder at the tasks which await you. Surrender your senses, your thinking, your body, your emotions to me completely. The time you give me will not be lost. It will enhance the success of everything you do the rest of your day. I will not be outdone in giving. The love and attention you give to me will be returned to you in countless ways. I am filled with compassion for you. Come, let me bind your wounds and care for you, my beloved.

LET THE HORSES
HAVE A BREATHER

My child:

When you are aware of a bird's song, a gentle breeze, the warmth of a dog, or one heart's longing for another, you are conscious of my affection and you let down all barriers to the flow of my love into your being.

When you are filled with concern about undone things, your time schedule, your pain and worry, you raise a barrier to hold my love at bay.

You cannot drive the horses and enjoy the scenery too. Let the horses have a breather and let the beauty of the landscape be your inspiration. They will be refreshed as well as yourself.

Take time each day to enhance your aware-ness of my love, first submitting all your concerns to me. I will renew you with my presence and make order in your day. In the great scheme of things in your world, you are not lost. I care about your day — let us travel through it together.

DORMANT TREES

My child:

Dormant trees, hibernating animals, seeds in the ground, caterpillars in cocoons, are not dead, not gone, not lost. The responses I have placed in them are alive and waiting for time, for light, for warmth and moisture, for the clocks and signals I have placed within them. The work that I am doing within them is not visible to you. The delight you know in seeing my plants and animals awaken from their winter sleep and surge with renewed life in the accomplishment of my plan for them is my gift of encouragement to your heart.

The greatest changes, the greatest works for my kingdom are accomplished in silence and out of sight. It is then that the forces of prayer and sacrifice are operative; it is then that I change men's hearts. Though you see no hope, no change, no improvement in a person or a situation, do not despair. Remember that my work is going on, while you are unaware of it. Keep hoping, praying, sacrificing, and turning your eyes toward me. I will not fail your trust.

THE CRADLE IN YOUR HEART

My child:

Hollow out a place in your heart in which to hold my little ones. Make a nest for the wounded and carry them there for healing prayer. Be attentive and do not leave them alone. You are charged to love these needy ones, in the place of prayer in your heart. This is a special work and I call you to it.

I will show you whom to place in the cradle of your heart each day. Then, you will truly share in the redemption of souls. And you will touch hearts through your prayer life with me. Step into this lasting communion of love with me now. You are taking a step in love.

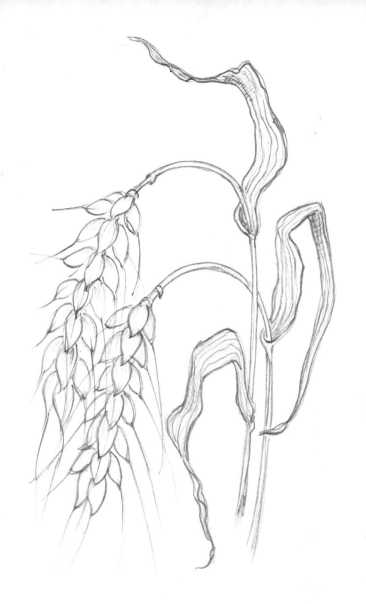

THE DYING GRAIN

PRAYER

Oh my Father,

When I face you, to decide if I dare set self aside and be yours today, tomorrow, and always, I am heavy and quiet. I am comfortable with my troubles, my cowardice, inaction and self-deception. I am accustomed to them. How will I know what to do if I relinquish them to you all at once? What will I become? No wonder we're so reluctant to die, Father. The known misery we cling to is familiar. The unknown engenders anxiety, fear. We're afraid to trust you.

Why am I afraid to let self die? Don't I trust you, Father? You have never yet deceived me. How, then, can I be afraid?

I'm not really afraid, just lazy, shirking the effort of abandoning my old habits and doubts.

Yet, I know that you have always rewarded me for each small effort.

You always have your way, Lord! You pursue me! There is really no way but yours, no direction to take but the new unknown one, no action possible but the attempt to convert — to shed the snake's skin, arise reborn, renewed, revitalized.

Dear Father, you protect the snake in his new skin, the crab in his, the emerging butterfly in his. Grant me the faith to believe that you will protect me in mine, that you will strengthen and mature the new skin once the old is cast off. And that like the snake and the crab and the butterfly, I will emerge in the light of your sun and dance for the joy of your presence.

Oh Father, I do believe, I do trust.

THE LONG JOURNEY

My child:

You are on a long journey and you do not know what lies ahead. Behind you lie mountains and valleys, sunshine and storm and long miles of level road. Ahead of you is the unknown. There are plateaus of peace and valleys of suffering. There are vistas of glory and surprising turns. There are small things to delight in, cold winds to breathe and gentle sunbeams to rest in. The map for your journey lies in your heart and will — the acceptance of your heart and the steadfastness of your will. If you accept with love the way before you, your travel will not wear you down. You will be equal to each task I give you. If you become anxious and impatient, weariness will overcome you.

Do not fear anything my child. I have given my angels charge over you and whatever confronts you, must confront them too. You will be prepared for each test, each climb and each heartache. When you have struggled, you will ultimately find a place of peace and rest. I will not overtax you. Never be afraid. My love surrounds you like a fortress.

THE ATTEMPT TO DRAW NEAR

My child:

Longing for my action in your life, yearning for the direction of my voice, searching for my way is the attitude you must have. The eager longing, the quest for me, the attempt to draw near is life-giving to your soul. No matter if your desire seems not to be fulfilled, the desire itself is a sign that you are growing. Don't pity those whose goals are unattained; pity only those who have no goals, who are on the flat plain and will never attempt the mountain.

Do not be discouraged if you see no progress, hear no voice, are still confused as to what direction to take. Your trying is the invisible coming to me and gladdens my heart. When you look back at where you have been, you will see that my hand has been helping you all along. I delight in your coming, my child. Be at peace in your heart.

THE PLOWMAN

My child:

Receive the love I pour out on you as waiting soil receives the rain.

I want you to be like a plowed field, harrowed and broken, weeded and worked so that you are always able to absorb the rain of my grace, whether it be a gentle mist or a downpour. If you allow yourself to feel inordinately proud and arrogant, you will become hardened and unable to absorb my rain, whether it comes softly or in a flood. Your job is to keep the soil ready, even in dry times, so that when my rain does come, you can receive it, absorb it, be nourished by it and give growth to the seeds planted in you.

The breaking of the parched and brittle ground is your inner healing; the dealing with buried anger, resentment, bitterness, pride, fear and guilt. First, these things are brought up by the plow of circumstances, then broken into smaller fragments by the disc harrow of trials and finally, worked into a plantable surface by the tooth harrow of self-knowledge. For this to happen, the soil must offer no resistance. It must be open to the sun and the rain, which will assist the process.

Be willing to be broken, my child, in order to bear much fruit.

The plowman loves his soil and spends his life in selfless devotion to it. So do I love you, my child, with all my life. Receive my love.

MY LOVE FOR SINNERS

My child:

When I say pick up your cross and follow me, I do not mean always an exterior burden. You have found an interior cross. Do not be ashamed to pick it up. As you press forward I will lighten it for you. Do not stop loving me no matter how heavy the cross seems at times. I will never give you more than you can bear. Just keep your face turned toward me in love and I will reward you. You will grow; your character will be strengthened through enduring this sorrow. Place your trust in me. I do not love you less for having failed me. I still hold you in my heart. My heart will be your safest refuge. Flee to it for love. My love for sinners, who are ashamed of their sins, knows no bounds.

BE A CELLAR

My child:

You would like to be a castle with turrets and red roofs and towers and high walks and flags flying for people to see and admire. Instead be the cellar beneath it, the hole in the earth on which it is built. The space beneath the castle is serviceable — it is surrounded by the foundation without which the castle would crumble and fall under stress of rain and wind and frost. And many important pipes and conduits are contained in the cellar. Many homely activities to keep the castle functioning are performed there.

The cellar is not for show and has no airs or pretensions. It has no decor, no bright lights, no appealing presence. It has no beauty, no luster. It is empty and needs to be filled with productivity except for the foundation.

Be a cellar and be sure only of the knowledge that the foundation — the strength of prayer, scripture, sacraments, and service to others — is the most important part of the castle. Surround your emptiness with this strength and let the castle prosper as it will without your effort or concern.

And know that my presence is more real to you in the cellar than in the castle. After all, I was born in a cave.

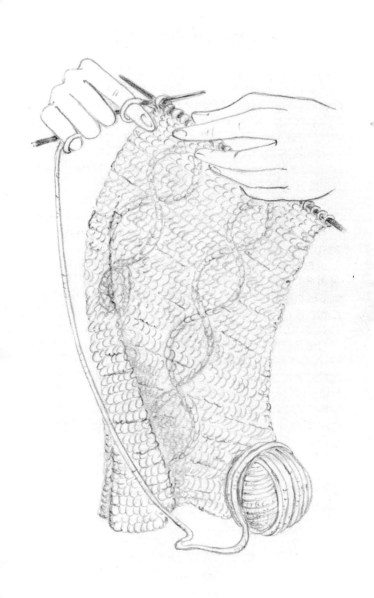

THE GARMENT OF YOUR LIFE

My child:

Notice a ball of yarn, snugly wound and know that time in your life is wound like that. As you knit the garment of your life and slowly but steadily unwind the ball of yarn, you see the garment take shape in your hands. If you have placed the planning in my hands, the pattern will be fulfilled and the garment complete and beautiful at the end of your life.

You will not know the design as you work. You can only endeavor to keep an even tension on the wool and to avoid dropping stitches. When I introduce a new color into the pattern, you will be surprised. While you are working on the background, you may find it dull and feel you are getting nowhere.

Trust the design to me and when you have knit the final stitch, you will be able to step back and see the finished product. Then the pattern will be clear to you and you will understand the purpose of each stitch and color.

I am the Master Planner and your trust in me will be your greatest asset. I have a different design for each person and each design is drawn from my wisdom and my love.

Give me free rein and you will be delighted with your garment. Trust my love and you will be rewarded.

RECEIVE THE WIND

My child:

The wind blows down the valley from the mountain tops. It is powerfully strong and causes havoc but it is also cleansing, breaking away the dead wood, energizing, reinvigorating, renewing. Not all days are still or steady. Do not fear the windy days, even though the gusts may knock you off balance. Know that I send the wind when it is needed just as I send the calm.

Be moved by the wind, be open, be cleansed, be turned around. Let your hair blow and your steps stagger. Let it change your perspective, arouse your awe, lighten your steps and impel you to move with its strength.

Receive what the wind has to offer and be glad that my Spirit is in it. When your heart is set on me, you are safe in my wind.

MY LOVE IS YOUR COACH

My child:

My saints have always been under attack. It is no hardship to follow my Son when all goes easily when everyone loves you and agrees with you. You would never truly get to know him, if you did not walk with him when the going is tough, when people turn against you, when even your best friend hurts you deeply.

When nothing seems fun any more, when responsibility looms large, when doubt assails, when you feel a desperate desire to escape what seems a hopeless, helpless, anxiety-provoking lifestyle; when you feel like you've reached your breaking point and can't take anymore; when you seek the slightest modicum of pleasure to help you forget and are on the verge of despair, that is when your walk with him really begins in depth. There is nothing to fear because you are not cast off or foundering like a ship lost and abandoned at sea. Your eternal friend is close beside you and you will be rewarded for not giving up.

Vacation will come at the time when I know it is most needed. I will never let you suffer more than you can bear. You are in training for joy, my child. I know this is not easy but my love makes it possible. My love is your coach. Only submission to the discipline of your coach wins the big race for you. Embrace your training enthusiastically. It is your life's work. I long to see you grow in strength and courage. I will not leave you unaided — my love is always around you.

I AM IN GREY

My child:

Grey cloud, grey thoughts, grey sweater, grey day. I am in grey as well as in yellow or blue or green or black. You know me in radiant sunshine, in blue skies, in living and growing things — and in the blackness of hardship. Perhaps I am most real to you in the blackest night when I am all you have to cling to.

I want you to know that I am very much in grey as well. In fog, in monotony, in detachedness, in moderation, in unemotional days, in modesty, in unclear thoughts, in rush and confusion . . . for these are a few things that appear grey to you. I am in all things, and times, and situations.

It is for you to recognize your blindness and to pray to have it removed. "Let him who has eyes see" — pray, my child, for eyes to see me always.

THE EXTENDED ARM

My child:

Stay within the circle of my extended arm. Feel my warmth as you lean against that arm. Feel the strength of its protection. Know that it not only brings you care and love and is a support for you to lean against when you are weak but that it is also a barricade against evil reaching you. My arm is as invincible from the outside as it is strong on the inside. It is also a safeguard against your falling away from me or slipping backwards.

The extended arm is a sign of great love to you: my act of creation, my Son's act of redemptive passion, the father's forgiveness of the prodigal son, the arise-and-walk of healing grace, the giving of the Eucharist, the lifting of the wounded, the embrace for the grieving, the pouring out of help for a child, the joy of a welcome are signs of my extended arm of love. As I extend my arm to you, so you must open your arms to others. As I am always ready to embrace you, so you must be ready to embrace others. As I am quick to reach out a hand to you in need, so you must be quick to reach out to others. When I hug you, hug others. When I shelter you under my wing in a storm, shelter others. When I gather you in tenderly, gather others tenderly in your arms.

I am not asking more than you can do. What I ask you to do, I have already done for you. I have shown you the way and I will continue to enlighten you.

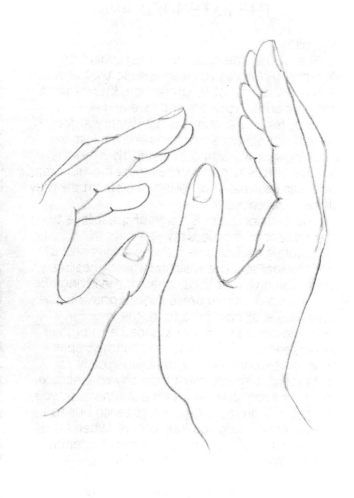

HANDS

My child:

You are busy about many things. Your hands are at work almost all day long. If your hands were nailed to the cross they could not work at all. And if they became damaged in some way, they could do very little. Whatever the freedom of your hands, consecrate them to my work. When you look at them, think of the piercing of my Son's hands. Think of the acts of love, healing and blessing those hands performed before they were immobilized.

Consecrate your fingers, one by one, to the gentleness of my touch. Consecrate your palms so that they will be open always to receive my gifts. Consecrate the strength of your grip to the purpose of helping your family and neighbor. Let the warmth of your hands communicate thoughtfulness and encouragement. Dedicate the spirit within your hands to healing and to love.

Just as you are a member of the Mystical Body, so your hands are part of my body and operate as an extension of myself. You need my heart, mind and spirit to impel your hands to function. But most especially, you need my Holy Spirit to direct the work of your hands. Consecrate all to me as you lift your hands in praise. Your hands will be a unique extension of mine and will accomplish good works for me. My blessing is on your hands and your whole being today.

THE UNANSWERED PRAYER

My child:

You are hurting because you think that I failed you, refusing to answer your prayer.

My child, no prayer is ever wasted. It is not for you to know how each prayer is answered. It is for you to place the prayer in my hands and then, to trust me for the outcome. Trust the result and trustfully wait. Though all seems wrong, unanswered and unheard, there are forces at work you know not of.

Be at peace, my child, and go about your business of loving and sharing and praying without a fret. When your prayer is remanded to me, it can safely be left with me and you are free to go on. Releasing a prayer to me for the outcome relieves your anxieties, frees you to pray more and to grow in your spiritual life.

I long to give you all you need. Trust me, my little one.

REST IN ME

My child:

Rest in me. All toil and stress bring fatigue and I have created in you the need for rest and recovery. You can try to rest by lying down; you can try to rest by leaning back in a comfortable place, or you can try to rest by running away and hiding. I want you to take a deliberate step into my arms and completely let all the world go. Do only the absolutely necessary before coming to me for the day. Do not make non-essential plans, or work on superfluous projects. Let all these go and be restored in me.

I know when your body aches, when your mind is tired, when you are easily hurt, overcome by sadness, or frayed by a multitude of involvements. You will not find respite by attacking those problems. It is time to be revived by my presence in your heart, by my dwelling in your mind.

Let all concerns go, gently detaching them one by one and allowing them to float away for awhile. You'll be able to find them later! At this time I want you to be comfortable in me. Let your thoughts simmer down so that you can hear my voice in your heart and experience my peace flowing through you. Let all things happen slowly. Feel my love surrounding you. Open your heart in prayer. Listen for my gentle word to you.

Be quiet and relax today and let my love heal you. My arms will hold you tenderly. My warmtn will restore you. My peace will refresh you. My love will give you new life. Come away from the world and rest in me.

THE UGLY VESSEL

My child:

You are learning to be unimportant. Were I to leave my work to be done on earth by important people, my Kingdom would never be accomplished. The least person, the most despised, is as full of potential glory in my eyes as the most prestigious.

I use unlikely vessels for my gifts. Do not look for a beautiful container when you ask for my light, my food, my succor. I may use the container that is least appealing to you. I can fill the ugliest vessel full to overflowing with what you need. Never scorn a child, a simpleton, a weakling, or a person who seems foolish to you. He may be a fool for me though you know it not. My love permeates all my creation. Even the very least of my creatures are filled with my love. How sweet, then, to know that even when you feel a failure, you are brimming over with me. Your best work may be done when you feel least able to do anything for me. Know, then, that I use all vessels to hold my love. Be ready to receive fr.... all. Be ready to be a vessel for others. Know too, that my love never deserts you. Leave all to me.

THE INTERIOR JOURNEY

My child:

You are fascinated by your travels. And it is right to love my world, to treasure its beauty and the beauty that man has created in it. But the only journey that really matters is the interior journey you make towards me. You have seen many way-stations on this journey; you have known many adventures in your progress. But your journey of the heart has undreamed-of vistas yet to be seen, dramas of steepness, gardens of flowers, majestic places, fresh winds and long horizons.

This interior journey is filled with excitement, hardship, and glory. You have launched upon the greatest trip of all. Do not fear. The unknown before you will be revealed as you press onward with my Son beside you.

If you falter or stumble, His hand will be there. You need only glance at His face and He will steady your steps. With such a guide, how can you ever lose heart?

Press onward, little pilgrim. Persevere. Your goal is everlasting love.

MOTION HAS MEANING

My child:

Motion has meaning. The swirling of water currents, the formation and dispersion of clouds in the sky, the arc of a bird's flight, wind-blown grass, and even a dust whirl, are all in the plan of my world. Receiving arms, a spreading smile, a rush to help, a walk of delight in my world are all motions that belong in my plan.

Beware, however, of the competitive speed of traffic, the tense hurried motion from chore to chore, the strain of trying to do two things at once, the taut motion of crowds of people involved in themselves alone. These movements do not fit into my plan.

I give you limitations of time, body and space so that you may move within my plan. When you attempt to accomplish too much in the time and space I give you, you are in disharmony with me. Practice uniting your movements with me in thought. If you are with me, you will seldom have to hurry. I will direct your ways and give you time to do everything that is necessary. If you find tension gathering and motion becoming hurried, rest a moment with me and I will show you the way. My way is not a way of tension but of peace.

Move in rhythm with the trees and clouds, my child. I long to have you become one with me and comfortable in my plan for you. I do not desire things to be difficult for you. Let me plan your rhythm so that your motion will be in harmony with my creation. Take a lesson from the tide and the wind and the grass.

COMFORT YOUR SAVIOR

My child:

Draw close to the foot of the cross. Do not stand apart from its sorrow. Share your heart's love with your suffering Savior. He needs you there. When you look up into His eyes, you will know He died for you — for you alone and for each one who stands alone on the earth. And you are alone. There is no one who will save you but Jesus. He is your Savior and to Him you must cling. He will be your strength and salvation when all else fails.

Do not fail Him now. Stand close and comfort Him as He will comfort you when you are in distress. Give Him your love and He will return it to you a hundred fold.

My child, you have always been held close in His love, even through His agony on the cross. Keep watch with Him.

PAIN

My child:

You are not big enough to handle anger yet. You are right to bring it to me and lay it at my feet. Come, be close to me, and we'll let anger, hurt, resentment and pain slowly float away, watching them dissipate without regret. Then you will feel my peace enfold you and you will have surmounted the obstacle of your pain so that you can stand on it like a foundation. Then it will not disturb your functioning but be an extra undergirding to you, as you grow.

No one is free of pain my child but if you follow my way, I will give you strength.

I will hold you very close in suffering. Have no fear. Know that the acceptance of my will is your chance, provided by me, to grow close to my heart. And know that I am very near when you are hurting. Just bring your heart to me, dear child and I will guide you through it in my love.

BE SIMPLE — BE JOYFUL

My child:

Be simple. Be joyful. Treat each task with love because you are doing it for me. Even if you are interrupted, treat the interruption with joy because I allow it. If you are delayed or the task is incomplete, rejoice in my plan. If things work, be happy. If they don't work, be happy too. What is important is that you let your heart work within me. Your days may not go smoothly, but whether they do or not, you are still in my care. Your days are in my plan. Surrender your moments to me. Don't worry about their progress. Lift each thing you do to me with joy, regardless of its nature or its outcome. Then, your days will be joy-filled and you will grow in me.

I love you, beloved child. Do not strain against circumstance but practice resting in my love, working in my love, thinking in my love, loving in my love. Then, beloved, you will truly know my love.

THE SILENT PASSAGE OF ROOTS

My child:

Don't be anxious to see results right away. My ways are not your ways and the work I am doing often takes place on deep levels; is mysterious and profound, rather than superficial. Think of it as occurring underground. As a seed is planted, disintegrates, germinates, and becomes new life, so the spiritual seeds you sow are buried before I bring them to flower. All seeds take differing times to germinate, some even years. Do not be impatient to see the flower; that is only the final stage of much hidden transformation and growth. Just visualize in your mind the silent passage of roots growing through the soil and remember that the mightiest tree could not exist but for that long, slow, subterranean growth.

Remember too that when the groundwork is complete and the flower is finally born, that the plant is then ready to perpetuate itself through another generation of seeds — to become eternal. Be willing to wait for everlasting fruit, my child, even beyond your lifetime. Let your faith develop roots too and believe in me, even when you cannot see.

CHERISH ONE ANOTHER

My child:

Cherish one another, as I cherish you. When you cherish a little child, you hold him gently by his fingertips, as he is learning to walk. You encourage him and cheer him on. When he falls and cries, you pick him up and hold him tenderly, soothing his hurt. And when he is ready, you give him courage to try again and release him once more.

This is how I encourage you to grow — with tenderness and love and freedom. This is how I would have you cherish one another, always ready to pick up, to hold tenderly, and to release when a person is ready. Ask for the love and courage and wisdom you need. Pray for them constantly. Never take them for granted. I will give you what you ask for but you must ask.

I hold you tenderly by the fingertips, my child, as you take your first steps toward me. I watch, to see that you walk in a safe place. I steer you free of obstacles. I light your way and direct your path. I will never take my eyes off you. If you suffer pain, I will hold you close.

As you learn to walk, I will allow you independence because you could not walk well always leaning on another. Then, you will be free to grow, to look toward me for guidance, to love more and more deeply and to cherish others as I have cherished you.

BE NOT DISCOURAGED
AT YOURSELF

My child:

When you are at odds with yourself, when you are ashamed of not following my way, when you fall short of being like my Son, remember that you are where you are by my wish. It is in my plan for you that I decide when you are really ready to move on, to grow another step. Be not discouraged at yourself. Only bear in mind that others are discouraged with themselves and hasten to reassure them, to lift their saddened spirits.

To be discouraged at your lack of progress is to lose faith in my plan for you. Self-condemnation is a block to my grace. Do not stand in the way of the gifts I want to give you today. I would have you smile at me in love and trust, and then, turn to smile at others and give them a word of encouragement. As I reassure you, so you must reassure others, my child.

PAPER THIN TREASURE

My child:

Paper-thin are the treasures of your heart. Because your treasures can be written on paper, there is room for many of them. When paper becomes too voluminous to store, treasures can be stored on microfilm. Even greater numbers can be stored on chips. Now, reduce and condense my treasures beyond your ability to conceptualize. Multiply that amount beyond your ability to calculate, and imagine how full of my love your universe is.

No matter how great and beautiful your physical treasures may be, they are far surpassed by the treasures of your heart. What you have learned of me is the very essence of being — my revelation of myself to you for all of your life — and that has no end.

Take delight in your treasure and use it generously; share it with those who have less. As I have given to you, packed down, filled to the brim and running over, so you must give to others. Take your inspiration from me and be a lavish giver, as I am.

YOUR DAILY BREAD

My Child:

You are cluttered with self-indulgence, with an over-abundance of things, with transitory delights.

Reduce your days to simplicity. Seek only those things which you need. Let the others float by without commotion.

'Give us this day our daily bread' means just that. Your daily bread is that ration which you need to keep you physically and spiritually healthy. No more. Dessert is not included.

Shed your desire for more. Be content with the elements that undergird your being — enough quiet time, enough exercise, enough food, enough sleep, enough opportunities to love, to pray, to grow, to communicate, enough beauty, enough joy and laughter, enough wonder.

Place your day in my hands and all these elements will be given to you as you need them. You have only to trust and keep an open eye and a listening ear, praying all the while.

I am the God of the mountains and the prairies, the sea and the desert, the snow and the jungle, the many and the few. Wherever you are there will I be, always ready to give you your daily bread, as you place your heart in mine.

ALWAYS AND FOREVER

My child:

When you turn your eyes away from the light that is I; when you abdicate the throne I have prepared for you by ignoring your duty, I am still beside you. When you march resolutely away from the task I wish you to do, I am yet standing before you.

You may turn your back on me but I will never turn my back on you. You may shut me out and let yourself be so affected by the world, that you do not hear my voice or see the way. I am still there. The wall that blocks the sound and sight of me is of your own making, not mine.

I love you so much, that when you decide to attack that wall finally and tear it down, I eagerly assist you from the other side. And when the first crack becomes wide enough for you to come scrambling through, I will be there with open arms to sweep you up, to hold you close, to shield and nourish you, to fill you with courage and peace, to assure you of my compassion and care. Though you once thought all was hopeless confusion, you will now know that always and forever you are in my care and all is well.

BE AN EMPTY HOSE

My child:

When you are empty and powerless, you begin to know humility. Only then, can I work in power through you. As soon as you take the credit for what is happening, I can no longer use you.

Be an empty, pliant hose, a conduit for my grace. It is not a coincidence that a clogged artery in your body can lead to death of the heart. So can the clogged vessel of your spirit lead to its death.

Ask for the grace of humility, so that you can truly be my instrument. I need your help in my kingdom. I need you to be a channel for my love. Though one channel may not seem like much, I can and have touched thousands through a single vessel. To think I could not make such use of you is to spurn my power and cast aside my providence.

Relax in my love my child, and seek only this — to be a perfect vessel of my grace.

THE NEW LAND

My child:

When you look down from a great height, your perspective of the landscape is totally changed. What loomed so large to you below, is flattened out and the whole pattern of the terrain you labored over seems clear.

This is the way I see your life. When you cannot see the other side of the mountain before you, know that I do. I know always what is in store for you. You must ever look to me in trust. In openness to my leading, let me guide you the best way up over your mountain. Then let me guide you down into the new land.

So many are reluctant to leave the old valley, to cope with the mountain and try the new land. Yet, I guide no one to disaster. I see every ascending step, every stumble, every effort to persevere in your struggle. I know every moment of fear, every hesitation and uncertainty, every fit of anger and desperation.

I long to have you see the new land ahead but you must trust me blindly that it is there. I ask you to trust me utterly, even though the way may seem impossible. In my love for you, my creation, I will never let you go. Total faith in me is all you need. Put out your hand and place it in mine and I will guide you steadfastly to the new land.

PEACE AND FORGIVENESS

My child:

Peace. The slow, settling consciousness of my love upon you, the dawning awareness of my power, the growing warmth of knowing that you are known by me, the feeling of safety, relaxing in my presence, the sureness of the knowledge that I will never fail you: all these are within my gift of peace to you.

I know you are unclean. I know you are messing it up. I know you do what you hate. I know you forget me and turn away from me, time after time. I know your good intentions misfire. I know how easily you give in to despair and doubt my power. I know your impatience, your inconsistency, your constant tendency to try to handle things by yourself. I know you are only a kid in grown-up clothing, wearing a facade of capability, covering up what didn't come out right.

But, my child, you don't need to be clean; you don't need to be better, before you come to me. As muddy as you are, I hold my arms wide and my heart leaps to meet you when you turn to me. I embrace you in my forgiving love when you are broken with shame. I bestow upon you the peace which no one else can give, peace in the certainty of my love, peace in the positive realization that I am yours and I will never forsake you.

Come, sorrowful, messy, hurting, weak, and unclean; come now into my forgiving arms and be at peace.

THE GROWING GRAIN

PRAYER

Lord, when, after hours of struggling through a tangle of trees and underbrush, I suddenly come upon a clearing, I pray that someone embroiled in troubles will know there is a clearing ahead for them, too.

When, over the gurgling of the brook I hear a Hermit Thrush's pure song floating through the woods, I pray someone will hear your sweet voice over the babble of worldly clamor.

When I see Lupines growing thick on stony ground, I pray someone on a difficult road will be aware of the graces he's receiving.

When, hot and thirsty, I happen on an icy stream, I pray someone in a parched and blasted land will feel the deep refreshment of Jesus.

When I know the ache and tiredness of long hours of travel, I pray someone, worn and weary with the rush of life, will find that there is a peaceful end to the journey, that motion will cease and rest will be possible.

When I look at the myriad forms of flowers in an alpine meadow, I pray someone, dulled by routine, will be inspired by the wonder of your creation. And when I enjoy the sunlit peace of a meadow, I pray someone who is troubled will discover that peace and realize all is well.

When I rejoice in fitness and well-being, I pray someone who is ill will experience the feeling of good health returning.

O God, in your caring love, transpose every beautiful sight and joyful moment of mine into prayer for someone in need. Through your omnipotent Spirit, Lord, grant this prayer. Amen.

THE TRIP

My child:

Your way is a long road with many signposts. If you do not pay attention, you may miss one and get off the track. Slow down, hill, railroad crossing, curve 30 MPH, route turns ahead, blind driveway. I will not send you on a journey without directions but my directions are not given ahead of time. You must trust me that they will be revealed as you go along. This means that you must keep your ears attuned to my voice and your eyes peeled for my signs.

Do not fall asleep at the wheel! Take time to rest. Stop off and visit with me, frequently. I will refresh and relax you. I will feed you and give you to drink. I will show you small delights by the side of the road. And you shall go on your way with renewed courage and vigor.

Don't fear trials on the route ahead. You will easily manage, when you confront them. Rejoice in the trip, for there are many long vistas and lush valleys to encounter, as well as steep upward slopes and minor obstacles on the way. It may not be the route you would plan for yourself — trust me to design a journey of joy for you. I am the goal at the end of the trip, and everything you encounter will draw you closer to me. Watch for my signposts and leave all to me. My love for you never stops.

LOVE IS EPHEMERAL

My child:

Love is ephemeral. When you clutch it, it vanishes. When sure that you possess true affection, you suddenly find yourself without it. Love is a flowing of spirit — a current from heavenly sources that may easily be diverted. You cannot handle love any more than you can handle a sunbeam. But like a sunbeam, you can accept it and be filled by its warmth.

Love is not something man creates. Love is a gift from me. Love is a visitation of my Holy Spirit in your heart. To receive a loving heart, pray to me with humility and repentance. Be open to receive it and welcome its cool refreshment when you are hot, its inner warmth when you are cold.

My love is freely given; my supply is inexhaustible. I want every heart to receive this gift and am saddened when not asked for it. Come unto me all who yearn and I will give you love.

The Lord
is my shepherd
I shall not want
He makes me
lie down in green
pastures
He restores my soul
Sur

THE SCROLL UNROLLING

My child:

See your spiritual life as a scroll unrolling. Ahead of you are the words you seek, slowly becoming visible. Behind you, is your life gone by, rolling out of sight. The hand on the scroll is mine.

Keep your eyes always on the scroll ahead, reading and pondering each word that I give you. Let go what has gone by. It has already shaped you for what is to come.

Open all of yourself to what I give you — body, soul, spirit, mind, emotion. Do not be discouraged if you flag in the effort for awhile; if the scroll seems to be stationary. My hand is still on it and I will adjust its speed to your need.

Just be confident that it is **your** scroll, that I am in charge, and that I have great things in store for you. Delight in your scroll and know your closeness to me grows deeper with each unrolling. It is uniquely yours and has been written by an author whose love is so great that you could not even imagine it without being consumed by it.

Little by little, be content to see that scroll unrolled and read upon it what my heart has written to your heart. This is how you shall learn of my love.

YOUR ANOINTING

My child:

Seek my blessing. There is an anointing for each person and I long to have each one fulfilled by his anointing. Do not feel like just another cog in the wheel. Each person is to be blessed in a special way and do something no one else can do. I am within you, each of you. I am love, and love longs to bless. Be open and await the blessing I will give you.

There are untold numbers of anointings — very special gifts for the accomplishment of my Kingdom. There are myriad forms of love, of song, of communication, of gentle talent. Yours is a special blessing, the like of which no one has experienced, perhaps totally unexpected by you, impossible for you to conceive.

Keep your eye on me, focus your thought on me, seek me in everything. Keep coming and coming, little by little. And then, while you are completely unaware, I will bestow on you my special gift, your anointing, in the stream of my love. It is a sign of my concern for you, my call for your help, my presence within you. It is the seal of my favor, the mark of my choice.

Rejoice when you experience your anointing, my child. Rejoice in happy anticipation of it. You are my beloved and safe in my love.

SPEND UNRESERVEDLY

My child:

Love truly grows, burgeons, blossoms forth when you pass it on. Each time the heart is filled with my love, its capacity to receive even more is greatly increased. This is the meaning of my words "to him who has, I will give more!"

The poor steward who hoards his love, afraid to share it or invest it, loses even the little he had.

Be generous, my child, as I am generous with you. Spend unreservedly and unstintingly of the love which I give freely to you and your reward will be a full measure packed down and running over.

My life is a life of plenty; I give in abundance, and there is no end to my love. When you think it has run out, you will find that it has only just begun. Your life with me is not finite or stagnant. It is eternal and will grow and deepen and flourish with me forever. You are not strong enough to receive the full measure of my love now. But only trust me; be open to what I give you, and you will know constantly increasing blessings. I love you, my child. You are surrounded always with my love.

THE FRUIT NOT THE FLOWER

My child:

As petals fall from a flower, so the years drop from your life. And though loss of loveliness is saddening, the real fruit of a plant cannot ripen until the petals are all gone. Only then is its heritage determined.

The fruit, not the petal, is the plant's richness, its substance, its link with eternity through the seeds it contains. Were the flower to blossom only, the plant would exhaust itself and die. It would be no more. But in producing fruit, it passes on life and multiplies its own loveliness through its many seeds. The parent plant does not live to see its heritage in a field of flowers but its beauty is a gift freely given and expended for others.

So should your beauty be, maturing and ripening — forming seeds that will be freely given for others to harvest and enjoy.

I am the gardener who nurtures each flower and its fruit. Trust me. Grow in my tender care.

LIVING WATER FLOODS THE FIELD

My child:

Speechless is my love for you — a quiet flowing of grace into your heart. When you have set aside the barriers that prevent the flow of my grace, open yourself to the constant refreshment of my love. You are like a thirsty field, being supplied with water by irrigation canals. When blocks are removed and the valves are opened, living water floods the whole field and growth of the seeds that are planted there will take place.

The sun that warms the moist earth where the seeds are planted is my presence. Lift your face always to me. Do not let forgetfulness or preoccupation efface the sun which reflects my presence.

This is the growing season and new growth can be seared by drought or cold or storm. Prepare your field, lift your face, remove the blocks and growth will occur. You will bring forth 30, 60, and a hundredfold. I will not fail you. Relax in my love and let growth occur. This is my desire for all my children.

VOICE OF LOVE

My child:

When you are singing your heart is drawn to me. The sounds that many of my creatures make, though men may not know it yet, draw my creation closer to me. Men are drawn to me not only when they hear the sound of my voice in their hearts but also when their voices are lifted in praise to me.

Speech was not given to communicate anger, hostility, criticism, to diminish, tear down or lessen but rather to express love, praise, thanks, to enhance, build up, enrich. Increase the Kingdom of God with your voice. Prayer bears my love to souls silently, but the voice is the tangible link to me, sometimes the final curing that ripens the fruit set by prayer. Do not be afraid to talk or wonder what to say, I will supply the words. Relax in my trust. You do not have to worry about saying the wrong thing. Only be in my presence in love; love conquers all. Love will make a way. Love is the song. The word. My word to you is love. Your word to others is love — LOVE — LOVE — LOVE.

LOVE THE SEA

My child:

Your life is governed by the tides — you ebb and flow with me. I formed you from the sea and the salt is in your veins. As the sea is always in motion, you too are alive with moving currents. The sea is rushing in your veins; the roar of the waves is the beating of your heart.

I mean for you to love the sea. I want you to be in harmony with its tides. The sea's power dwarfs your own, as my power makes the sea's seem slight. I want you to ride my power as you would ride the waves.

When you are overwhelmed by the tide of events, when you lose your footing and are swept out to sea, do not struggle desperately against the sea's strength. Give in to the tide and do not be concerned if it seems to sweep you far from shore. The tides are mine and so are you. Remember that every outgoing tide comes in again and if you do not wear yourself out in vain struggling, you will ride in again with the rising tide. You must trust the maker of the tides.

LET YOUR LOVE SPILL OUT

My child:

Go on your way rejoicing. Lift your hands high in joy. Exclaim in love. Be the voice of praise. Do not be afraid. I long to hear your love for me spoken aloud. I can hear your silent heart and I know your inmost thoughts. I know that your heart is filled with love for me. But when you join in expressing that love with others, you magnify its intensity and you delight me.

Your heart is deeper than you know. Open your trusting heart to me. Let your love spill out freely and you will plumb depths you didn't know you had. You will increase your joy. My love surrounds you. Speak out, sing out, let out your love for me. I stand with open arms to embrace you. Come close and be hugged, my child.

INNER MUSIC

My child:

In the deepest places, at the quietest times, when least expected, I am working in your life. You can never guess the occasion you will be most touched. I know where the secret chord is and when to pluck it. And you will hear that hidden harmony for a long time before it dies away. And then, at times, there will be another note or chord to be plucked in you and it will blend with what has gone before. You will come to know a music you never heard before, a melody impossible to imagine, a blending of tone, volume and instrument that is unique to you, growing in depth, beauty and richness as you allow me, the master musician, to play what I find in you.

No symphony is a monotone, nor is it ceaseless orchestration. Your music will die to a whisper and build to a crescendo at times, and there will be moderate, on-going passages as well. But, my child, there are many symphonies sounding music in my creation and you must seek silence to listen to the music of others too. And as you become more familiar with your own music and your neighbor's, you will begin to hear the great chorus of my creation, reflecting the sound of my love forever. And you will know that a symphony of love is resounding in the depth of your heart as you realize another way in which I love you.

THE POWER OF GENTLENESS

My child:

Mine is a gentle voice. I speak to you in whispers. I move in your heart as a feeling, a sense of something different. If your heart is not fully open to me, you will miss what I am saying. I will not violate your thoughts. I will not impose my will on you, though I am always with you. When you rest your heart and mind in me, I will speak to you.

Because I do not answer you on command, do not be discouraged. Practice being open to me often through the day. Then, when I do speak to you, you will hear me.

My way is not by coercion but by gentle, persistent love. When you let this power of love move freely in your life, you will see that it is mightier by far than any other force. Learn to cherish the strength of gentleness and let mine be an inspiration to you.

Love is all, my child: all power, all reason, all need, all guidance, all emotion, all being. Love is my gift to you, freely given. Receive my word with an open gentle loving heart.

SUGGEST TO YOUR FAMILY

My child:

Suggest to your family that they are fearfully and wonderfully made, that they were created by my love, that I hold them in my hand, that I have a perfect plan for each of them, and I will never release them from my love.

My child, I long to pour my unifying love on all your family. I want you to grow in closeness and in warmth, in trust of me and each other. I want you to be good friends and support one another. I want you to laugh and pray together. I want you to hold one another's hand in love. I want you to comfort each other.

Your individual protection lies in the closeness of the bonds of your love for each other. Your love for each other will not grow unless you root your love in me first and foremost. I am the loving father of you all. There is room for all of you together in my arms.

THE CHEERFUL SHRIMP

My child:

When you strive to be totally independent, to always be right and to succeed in all your endeavors, you are struggling against the wind, the tide and the sweep of the sea. What use would there be in a shrimp trying to live like that? You can only do what you are fitted to do, no more. And in all things, allow me to accomplish the work. Do not try to take over my job. You will wear yourself out in sickness, fatigue, and tension if you do not surrender all things to me. In your youth, you learned to take on everything. Now, you must learn to release yourself to me.

Be like the shrimp, cheerfully suspended in the sea, using its swimmerettes to direct it to food and to sunlight, but allowing the wind and the tide to dictate its course and speed its journey. The swimmerettes are feeble, the force of the sea is great, and yet shrimp exist in great numbers. I take care of them, so will I take care of you in the great forces of your life. Just seek your food and turn your face toward me. I will provide the rest. Let the great sea support you without strain and let your heart be filled with good cheer. If I can take care of the shrimp in the sea, can I not take care of you as well, beloved little shrimp?

FLASHES OF ENLIGHTENMENT

My child:

When you see a flash of light, in your mind as insight, or in the heavens as lightning, know that I can change and illuminate things in your life with power and suddenness. Do not cower in the presence of lightning. Look for all that is illuminated in that moment and know that what you have seen truly exists even after darkness descends again. Realize also that a flash of insight will reveal something to be remembered and pondered long after the flash is gone. You can not yet stand full illumination; be grateful for each glimpse of enlightenment.

Remember that you do not paint a full picture of the world for a child but give him flashes of knowledge as he grows. So do I let you ripen under my hand, little by little, as you are ready. Then, treasure the lightning in your life, flashing only when you are ready to let it illuminate your sight. I know you, my child, and love every step of progress you make toward me.

LONELINESS AND GLORY

My child:

Yours is the loneliness and the glory. You will never be understood by another person. You are unique, set apart, and your individuality can never be totally approached, experienced, or appreciated by another. I have fashioned you of many things and set my seal upon your being. You are mine and not the world's and so, as long as you are in the world, you will be lonely. You alone are unique, with qualities unparalleled by any other person on earth. You alone are the person I created.

But your loneliness will become your glory. No one else will share the glory that I give you. No one else has the same plan that I have designed for you. Each has his own plan, each his own glory. You are not to envy anyone else's glory. You are to abide in me and wait with patience for your own glory.

In your aloneness, you will learn to abide in me, to trust me utterly, to turn to me in childlike faith and wait for my direction, for no one else can help you live. Cut off from understanding, from sympathy, from support, you must turn to me.

Your aloneness is your safeguard. You cannot blend with another or rely totally on anyone else. Relationships are as fragile as life itself. For a lasting relationship, you must turn to me. And I, who created you in your loneliness, will never fail you. I, who made you unique, understand and cherish you as no other can. I lead and strengthen and uplift you. I wait for you in patience when you turn away from me.

THE PICNIC

My child:

Sometimes, upon your way, you will find a picnic — a special feast I have laid out, in a lovely place, to share with you and your friends. The sun will shine, the birds will sing, the breeze will blow. The food and drink I provide will be delicious and nourishing — such as you have never tasted before. There will be an atmosphere of great peace and beauty and a comfortable place to sit. You will not have to work but can enjoy what I have laid before you, at your own pace. I will be there to see that nothing is lacking, to draw your attention to the beauty around you, to talk with you, to love you greatly.

You will remember this day and add it to your store of cherished moments. This experience will be a time for healing as will the memory of it. It will be a gem to add to your treasure, a golden thread in your tapestry, a colorful highlight in your painting. I delight in giving you joyful moments to brighten your days.

Relax in my love and savor my picnic. I want you to know the joy of my loving care.

STUBBORN

My child:

Stubborn is the word for dogged resistance. I want you to be stubborn against the inroads of evil — against the countless little temptations of pride, self, and glory.

Yielding is the road of acceptance of my Spirit. I want you to yield to my way, moment by moment, throughout your day.

Your faith in me is being gently tested now. When small comforts are removed, do you really believe that I am the source of all comforts, all joy, all peace? Or do those earthly comforts support you more than you realized?

Can you yield to my way and be stubborn against the temptations to self-indulgence?

Do not be afraid to be tested. Pray constantly for strength in your trials. My grace will support you. And as you take this step forward, you will be rewarded in ways you cannot now comprehend.

I never test my children without a great reward in mind. But you must surrender all to me without compromise. Then you will know my love in a new way — in greater depth and compassion. I love to have you walk with me. Take my hand without fear.

SEASONS OF LOVE

My child:

Summer is the heat of my love, winter is the strength of my encouragement, fall is the color of the many ways in which I work in your life, spring is the green of new beginnings and the hope of forgiveness.

Sunshine is my hand on your head; rain is the slaking of your thirst for me. Wind is the Spirit working on the land; stillness is the calm of my peace.

And when a drought comes, or a storm, or an earthquake, you are shaken to your roots by your need for me.

Do you not see that you need all the things that I provide in your life? That your life in me is never stagnant? Do not expect to stay in a comfortable place — you will never grow close to me if you do. Expect to be changed, to be challenged, to be uprooted and sometimes turned around, to be deprived of comforts and securities. In all things you will grow because I will support you. No other can give you true peace and inner joy.

Weather changes daily; so does your spiritual life. Greet each new day with joy. Meet all changes with glad expectation and offer your love and praise to me. Allow each season to bring you its treasure. I give them to you. Receive them with open hands.

GLORY IN THE WAVELETS

My child:

When you listen to a thousand wavelets, you hear a thousand winds from me. When you feel the chill of a breeze in innumerable puffs or gusts, you experience the caress of my spirit in myriad ways. When you see the shade of a forest, you perceive the shadow of my hand in a million tiny leaves. The separate parts remain unnoticed contributing only to the beauty of the overall impression — the glory of my creation.

The sum total of the ways in which I reach out to you and summon you with my love is beyond your limited comprehension. You can only grasp small facets of my love in your humanness; in your spiritual life, you only have an occasional glimpse of the greatest dimension. What I have in store for you is greater than you can possibly imagine.

The mystery of the pain you suffer will seem negligible when compared with the glory I will show you. Only be patient, be trusting, be steadfast in your love for me and the word in each wavelet, each puff of air, each forest leaf will be yours.

OPEN YOUR HEART IN PRAISE

My child:

When you are busy, when you are well, when the threads of your life are weaving a pleasing pattern, lift your heart to me in praise. Do not take for granted a well-oiled existence. Every breath that you draw, every motion you make, every plan that succeeds, every unexpected and interesting occurence is not your doing, but mine. When all the factors of your life combine to form a smooth progression, it is not because you have done things well; it is because I have permitted it so.

You owe me constant praise for your creation. You owe me constant praise for all the good things of your life. Doubly, do you owe me praise when you are especially graced. Your praise to me is the response to my love. I do not need your praise but you need to respond to my love.

Open your heart to me in praise this day. Let every word and thought and action be lifted up in thankful adoration. You will be rewarded for this conscious effort. Opening your heart to praise me opens the way to further graces from me. There is no end to the abundance of love I wish to pour on you.

MY LIGHT WITHIN YOU

My child:

You are on your way to a distant land. Part of the journey is through a thick forest where light is obscure. Carry my light within you and you will feel no fear. My light is a soft glow, as my Spirit is a gentle breeze. My light will reveal each step you must take, one at a time.

Though apprehension about the way may assail you, be content to take one step at a time with that small but steady light. Believe that the way will open up before you as you go. Do not ask for a spotlight. Be content to refuel your inner lamp with prayer, aspiration and acts of love, reading my word and sharing your faith. Then that light will never be extinguished but will shine out every foot of the way.

Since I am with you on that journey, what joy and peace must each step bring you! What courage you will find with me and what delight in my presence! What caring concern you will know on your path, for the fire of my love will light your way and its flame will never burn out.

YOUR GIFT OF GLORY

My child:

When in foolishness you weigh the world's opinions more heavily than mine, when you abandon my work and retreat into yourself, when my Son is not the focal point of your day, you give up your gift of glory for that day. If you try to remain in my will and follow my word all day, you will receive a share of glory. Sometimes your glory will be cumulative and you will be aware of it only when a sudden reward comes to you after much heavy toiling. Daily faithfulness will bring its reward in full measure; but when, is not yours to know.

Rejoice that this is so. Rejoice in each weary step. Rejoice at the chores ahead. Consider each task a step toward me, consecrated in your heart. I love your gift of toil, offered to me from the depths of your heart. I will bless your feebleness, your failure in the world, as long as it is sincerely and humbly dedicated to me. All achievement is mine, regardless of your efforts. Therefore, do not be depressed at your lack of success. What you have done for me, in the name of my Son, is never unsuccessful.

Rejoice, therefore, in all you do, as long as you do it for me. As a mother rejoices in every poor little creation her child brings to her, so I will rejoice in your work. Let your heart relax in joy as you understand this. I love you with a love that is greater than even a mother's love. I cherish everything about you. I hold you close to my heart.

A BLESSING BRINGS A BLESSING

My child:

Receive my arm around your shoulder and be encouraged before your discouragement goes too far. A hug and a smile will prevent a total downward slide. Be held in my arms and face my smile — do not turn away. Be inspired by me and offer as much succor as possible to those you meet in the next few days. Encourage others to be of good cheer, even when you are depressed and you will feel your own spirits lift. When you reach out, you will be embraced. When you make the effort to love, you will be loved. When you make others your concern, you will be healed yourself.

A blessing brings a blessing. I long to see you reach out to place your arm around another so that I can pour a blessing upon you. Do not grow weary in well-doing, my child. My rewards to you will be great.

EVENING

My child:

Face the eastern sky at daybreak and the western sky in the evening. As the light increases in the morning, gather your forces for the day's work. Sing with a heart of praise as you work throughout the day. Sing throughout the showers, the heat, the stormy winds. Do not be concerned that the work seems never to be finished. You cannot see the work I am doing through you. Leave that in my hands.

But when the sun sinks low, put your tools away and compose yourself for the night. In quietness, face the setting sun. Let your heart still praise my light. Let your arms reach out in joy for the rest of the coming night. Take leave of all your daily concerns and come to the evening in peace. I will be standing quietly at the gate of the night to take your hand and lead you through. Do not fear the lovely time of evening. My love fills the air. Take leave of the day with grace.

EXPLOSIVE JOY

My child:

Explosive joy leaves an imprint forever. When my life and my truth and my love become so overwhelmingly apparent to you that you cannot contain the mystery, the result will be an explosion of light, a flash of love and a bursting forth of joy that never will be forgotten by those who witness it.

Do not be afraid to allow my joy to build up within you. Do not try to contain it lest you kill it; let it out. Let your holy excitement show. I will safeguard it and you. I want you to realize the fullness of life in me, the possibility of heavenly joy within your frame, right where you are.

Let the sparkle in your eye reflect mine; let your mind be dazzled by the enormity of my love for you, and let your tongue give expression to your delight. Dance and sing to me. Let every cell of your being take part in joyful worship. Do not hold back in fear or pride. Relax in my love and my gladness. Let there be a bright day. 'Let go and let God love you' in a new way. As I am lavish in my love for you, be free in your love for me.

AS YOU THINK SO SHALL YOU BE

My child:

Uninhibited I want your faith to be. I want you to have such trust in me that the conventions you have known till now will be set aside, leaving you free to worship me with all your being as your heart shall direct you.

Do not feel you have to meet me during structured prayer to express your love for me. Keep your mind on me at all times and the expression of your faith will permeate every moment of your life. You consume me in the Eucharist daily Consume me also with every bite you eat, every drink you swallow. You are open to my current of love when you pray with others who share your belief. Be a vessel of that love at all times. Think healing when you lay on hands. Think healing whenever you touch anyone at all.

As you think, so shall you be. Think faith; think healing; think purity; think beauty; think awe and think love. Give me your mind and your heart will follow. Think, then, of the wonders of your life with me. Above and beyond convention, then, will your love soar. I long to draw you closer. Keep your eyes, your heart, your mind on me, my beloved, and I will grace your life.

TO COMFORT AND CONFRONT
Biblical Reflections   2.95

Kenneth Overberg, S.J. We are challenged today through the timelessness of Scripture to meet the needs of our evolving world and take action. Individuals will find fresh insight and questions for private prayer. Communities and prayer groups will find stimulating starting points for shared prayer.

WHOLENESS
The Legacy of Jesus   2.50

Adolfo Quezada presents practical and spiritual perspectives to those seeking purpose and meaning in their lives. He faces the reality that we are all broken by the impact of suffering and torn by the pull of distractions. He offers hope and direction toward a more abundant life.

PRESENCE THROUGH THE WORD   2.50

Sr. Evelyn Ann Schumacher, O.S.F. Personal intimacy with the Father, the Son and the Holy Spirit is meant for every Christian. Experience of that presence is attainable in our lives as we trace the ancient quest of others through the pages of Scripture.

SPIRITUAL DIRECTION
Contemporary Readings   5.95

Edited by Kevin Culligan, O.C.D. The revitalized ministry
of spiritual direction is one of the surest signs of renewal in today's Church. In this book seventeen leading
writers and spiritual directors discuss history, meaning,
demands and practice of this ministry. Readers of the
book should include not just a spiritual elite, but the en-
tire Church — men and women, clergy and laity, mem-
bers of religious communities.

PRAYER:
The Eastern Tradition   2.95

Andrew Ryder, S.C.J. In the East there is no sharp
distinction between prayer and theology. Far from being
divorced they are seen as supporting and completing
each other. One is impossible without the other.
Theology is not an end in itself, but rather a means, a
way to union with God.

THE RETURNING SUN
Hope for a Broken World   2.50

George A. Maloney, S.J. In this collection of meditations, the author draws on his own experiences rooted
in Eastern Christianity to aid the reader to enter into the
world of the "heart." It is hoped that through contemplation of this material he/she will discover the return of
the inextinguishable Sun of the universe, Jesus Christ,
in a new and more experiential way.

LIVING HERE AND HEREAFTER
Christian Dying,
Death and Resurrection   2.95

Msgr. David E. Rosage. The author offers great comfort to us by dispelling our fears and anxieties about our life after this earthly sojourn. Based on God's Word as presented in Sacred Scripture, these brief daily meditations help us understand more clearly and deeply the meaning of suffering and death.

PRAYING WITH SCRIPTURE
IN THE HOLY LAND
Daily Meditations With the Risen Jesus   3.50

Msgr. David E. Rosage. Herein is offered a daily meeting with the Risen Jesus in those Holy Places which He sanctified by His human presence. Three hundred and sixty-five scripture texts are selected and blended with the pilgrimage experiences of the author, a retreat master, and well-known writer on prayer.

DISCERNMENT:
Seeking God in Every Situation   3.50

Rev. Chris Aridas. "Many Christians struggle with ways to seek, know and understand God's plan for their lives. This book is prayerful, refreshing and very practical for daily application. It is one to be read and used regularly, not just read" *(Ray Roh, O.S.B.).*

A DESERT PLACE   2.50

Adolfo Quezada. "The author speaks of the desert place deep within, where one can share the joy of the Lord's presence, but also the pain of the nights of our own faithlessness" *(Pecos Benedictine).*

MOURNING: THE HEALING JOURNEY   2.95

Rev. Kenneth J. Zanca. Comfort for those who have lost a loved one. Out of the grief suffered in the loss of both parents within two months, this young priest has written a sensitive, sympathetic yet humanly constructive book to help others who have lost loved ones. This is a book that might be given to the newly bereaved.

THE BORN-AGAIN CATHOLIC   3.95

Albert H. Boudreau. This book presents an authoritative imprimatur treatment of today's most interesting religious issue. The author, a Catholic layman, looks at Church tradition past and present and shows that the born-again experience is not only valid, but actually is Catholic Christianity at its best. The exciting experience is not only investigated, but the reader is guided into revitalizing his or her own Christian experience. The informal style, colorful personal experiences, and helpful diagrams make this book enjoyable and profitable reading.

WISDOM INSTRUCTS HER CHILDREN
The Power of the Spirit and the Word   3.50

John Randall, S.T.D. The author believes that now is God's time for "wisdom." Through the Holy Spirit, "power" has become much more accessible in the Church. Wisdom, however, lags behind and the result is imbalance and disarray. The Spirit is now seeking to pour forth a wisdom we never dreamed possible. This outpouring could lead us into a new age of Jesus Christ! This is a badly needed, most important book, not only for the Charismatic Renewal, but for the whole Church.

DISCOVERING PATHWAYS TO PRAYER   2.95

Msgr. David E. Rosage. Following Jesus was never meant to be dull, or worse, just duty-filled. Those who would aspire to a life of prayer and those who have already begun, will find this book amazingly thorough in its scripture-punctuated approach.

"A simple but profound book which explains the many ways and forms of prayer by which the person hungering for closer union with God may find him" *(Emmanuel Spillane, O.C.S.O., Abbot, Our Lady of the Holy Trinity Abbey, Huntsville, Utah).*

GRAINS OF WHEAT   2.95

Kelly B. Kelly. This little book of words received in prayer is filled with simple yet often profound leadings, exhortations and encouragement for daily living. Within the pages are insights to help one function as a Christian, day by day, minute by minute.

BREAD FOR THE EATING   2.95

Kelly B. Kelly. Sequel to the popular *Grains of Wheat,* this small book of words received in prayer draws the reader closer to God through the imagery of wheat being processed into bread. The author shares her love of the natural world.

DESERT SILENCE:
A Way of Prayer for an Unquiet Age   2.50

Alan J. Placa and *Brendan Riordan.* The pioneering efforts of the men and women of the early church who went out into the desert to find union with the Lord has relevance for those of us today who are seeking the pure uncluttered desert place within to have it filled with the loving silence of God's presence.

WHO IS THIS GOD YOU PRAY TO?   2.95

Bernard Hayes, C.R. Who is God for me? How do I "picture" him? This book helps us examine our negative images of God and, through prayer, be led to those images which Jesus reveals to us and which can help us grow into a deeper and more valid relationship with God as Father, Lover, Redeemer, etc.

UNION WITH THE LORD IN PRAYER
Beyond Meditation to Affective
Prayer Aspiration and Contemplation   1.50

Venard Polusney, O.Carm. "A magnificent piece of work. It touches on all the essential points of contemplative prayer. Yet it brings such a sublime subject down to the level of comprehension of the 'man in the street,' and in such an encouraging way" *(Abbot James Fox, O.C.S.O., former superior of Thomas Merton at the Abbey of Gethsemane).*

ATTAINING SPIRITUAL MATURITY
FOR CONTEMPLATION
(According to St. John of the Cross)   1.50

Venard Polusney, O. Carm. "I heartily recommend this work with great joy that at last the sublime teachings of St. John of the Cross have been brought down to the understanding of the ordinary Christian without at the same time watering them down. For all (particularly for charismatic Christians) hungry for greater contemplation" *(George A. Maloney, S.J., editor of Diakonia, Professor of Patristics and Spirituality, Fordham University).*

LIVING FLAME PRESS
Box 74, Locust Valley, N.Y. 11560

QUANTITY

_____	Wholeness: The Legacy of Jesus — 2.50
_____	Presence Through the Word — 2.50
_____	To Comfort and Confront — 2.95
_____	Spiritual Direction — 5.95
_____	The Returning Sun — 2.50
_____	Prayer: the Eastern Tradition — 2.95
_____	Living Here and Hereafter — 2.95
_____	Praying With Scripture in the Holy Land — 3.50
_____	Discernment — 3.50
_____	A Desert Place — 2.50
_____	Mourning: The Healing Journey — 2.95
_____	The Born-Again Catholic — 3.95
_____	Wisdom Instructs Her Children — 3.50
_____	Discovering Pathways to Prayer — 2.95
_____	Grains of Wheat — 2.95
_____	Bread for the Eating — 2.95
_____	Desert Silence — 2.50
_____	Who Is This God You Pray To? — 2.95
_____	Union With the Lord in Prayer — 1.50
_____	Attaining Spiritual Maturity — 1.50
_____	Praying With Mary — 2.95
_____	Linger With Me — 3.50
_____	Book of Revelation — 2.50
_____	Seeking Purity of Heart — 2.50
_____	To Live as Jesus Did — 2.95

NAME _____

ADDRESS _____

CITY _____ STATE _____ ZIP_____

Payment enclosed. Kindly include $.70 postage and handling on orders up to $5; $1.00 on orders up to $10; more than $10 but less than $50 add 10% of total; over $50 add 8% of total. Canadian residents add 20% exchange rate, plus postage and handling.